Adapting working hours to modern needs

# Adapting working hours to modern needs

The time factor in the new approach
to working conditions

D. Marić

International Labour Office   Geneva

ISBN 92-2-101658-7 (limp cover)
ISBN 92-2-101659-5 (hard cover)

First published 1977

ILO publications can be obtained through major booksellers or ILO local offices in many countries, or direct from ILO Publications, International Labour Office, CH-1211 Geneva 22, Switzerland. A catalogue or list of new publications will be sent free of charge from the above address.

Printed by La Concorde, Lausanne, Switzerland

FOREWORD

Over the past two decades standard hours of work have been progressively reduced in industrialised countries. At the same time, improved education and living standards have led to more widespread concern with the quality of life among those working in big cities, and more recently there have been new developments in the distribution of working hours over the week and year.

These are of considerable interest in one of the major fields (i.e. conditions of work and life) in which the ILO is required to collect and disseminate information. The present volume supplements information given in an ILO study published in 1975 on hours of work in industrialised countries.[1] It is also relevant to the objectives of the proposed international programme for improving working conditions and the working environment at present under discussion in the Governing Body of the International Labour Office.

Since the current developments are so recent, the present volume does not give a detailed description of the approaches in the different countries. It is intended as an outline of new trends in the pattern of working time that have emerged in industrialised market-economy countries, for readers with a general interest in present-day labour problems.

The first chapter describes the new attitudes to the allocation of the individual's time in modern societies. The second shows how the reduction of standard hours created conditions for innovations in the arrangement of working time. The next six chapters deal with the compressed working day and week, staggered schedules, flexible working hours, part-time employment and improvement of the annual pattern; indicating some advantages and disadvantages reported and factors that must be considered in introducing and operating such schemes. The wider question of flexibility in the lifetime distribution of working time is referred to in a concluding note.

---

[1] Archibald A. Evans: Hours of work in industrialised countries (Geneva, ILO), 1975.

## CONTENTS

# I. NEW TRENDS AND ATTITUDES

## Significance of the time factor

The problem of working hours has until recently always been seen in purely quantitative terms. The aim has been to reduce the total time spent at work: (a) directly, by setting standard hours and overtime limits per day and week, and (b) indirectly, by prescribing spells of free time of varying length over longer periods of up to a year, in the form of public holidays and vacation leave.

While this approach is still useful in concrete cases, it is no longer adequate for present-day conditions. Modern developments have made it necessary to consider the qualitative aspects of the pattern of working hours, in the light of new thinking on the subject. What are needed now are ways of working less hours, differently and better, so as to achieve - without detriment to production and productivity - a balance between work, rest and leisure that meets the needs of the individual and of the community. This has involved analysis of working conditions and of the physical, economic and social environment of work, and the results have brought a new awareness of the importance of the time factor.

Since industrialisation began, the individual has increasingly been forced to surrender control of his time and, as a result, working time has had to be quantified in order to set a fair price for it. We now see that this cannot be done in monetary terms alone. The well-worn saying that "time is money" has fallen out of use, since it considers only what an individual earns - but not what he sacrifices - by working for a given time.

This brings us to a further question: what does a worker's pay really represent? Whether the criterion is muscular, mental or nervous effort, skill or know-how, the remuneration is always the result of multiplying the physical or mental qualifications by a time coefficient: time spent working, time devoted to vocational training or time lost at work - this last element representing a loss of "living time". Looked at in this way, remuneration clearly embodies an element of compensation for loss of time. The time dimension is now an inherent part of an individual's conditions of work and the main factor in the constantly rising social cost.

As a result, people are beginning to be conscious of how their time is spent, and to want to exercise choice in using it as profitably, agreeably and sensibly as possible.

For those living today, time means something radically different from time in the olden days. Work was then spread over the hours of daylight, without a set timetable. The human time-pattern corresponded to the alternations in nature and to human psychological and biological needs.

All this has been changed by industrialisation. Our way of life today follows a job and production engineering model that favours productivity at the expense of the natural needs and deeper motivations of the individual. We are reaching a point where the pattern of working hours ceases to correspond to human physiological and biological rhythms, since machines can function regardless of the natural divisions of time. Time is becoming a scarce and

**there**fore more costly factor and is divided up into ever-smaller
segments.  As Pierre Naville puts it, it is now the prize in a
bitter conflict between working for somebody else and working for
oneself and the whole community.[1]

Two other factors have contributed to the startling increase
in the value of the time factor.  It is one of the parameters in
measuring productivity, and we are only too aware of the priority
given to this in modern industrial societies.  At the same time,
many kinds of work are unpleasant and the price for time spent on
them is accordingly increasing.  The price may be paid in cash or,
when a given level of prosperity is attained, in the form of extra
time off.  As Grossin has pointed out, the reason why workers hand
over control of their working days is that they want fuller enjoyment of their non-working time, which is for them a period of
"de-alienation".[2]

## Reorganising the use of time

Technological progress, the development of large-scale production, and division of labour with the specialisation and assembly-
line methods to which it leads, have impoverished the worker's
relationship to his work.  The work process is often broken down
into simple and constantly repeated operations so that the worker
has no real feeling of contributing to the final product or result.
Work is consequently unsatisfying and there are increasing signs
of discontent.  Fatigue now tends to be nervous rather than
physical as formerly, and may disturb the individual's psychoso-
matic health, emotional life, and powers of attention and thought.
The whole process is one of increasing alienation, attributable to
two main causes:  dissatisfaction with the actual tasks involved
in the job, which give no scope for self-fulfilment, and dissatisfaction with extraneous factors, such as the physical conditions,
supervision, the state of labour relations, etc.[3]

Now, employee alienation represents labour's share of the
social cost of a given activity.  In some cases it is shown by
passive resistance:  lateness, absenteeism, high labour turnover
and inattentiveness;  in others, by aggressive behaviour such as
deliberate waste, threats, violence or quarrelsomeness in daily
work.[4]

---

[1] Pierre Naville, in the introduction to William Grossin:
Le travail et le temps (horaires, durées, rythmes) (Paris, Editions
Anthropos, 1969), p. VIII.

[2] Grossin: Le travail et le temps, op. cit., p. 150.

[3] See Laurent Bélanger:  "Les formes d'aménagement des temps
de travail", in L'aménagement des temps de travail (Quebec,
Département des relations industrielles de l'Université Laval,
1974), pp. 25-26.

[4] Union des industries métallurgiques et minières:  "Etats-
Unis - Comment combattre l'aliénation à l'usine", in Documentation
étrangère (Paris, Dec. 1972), Annex 1, pp. 2-3.

In spite of the changed working environment and social climate, there is still a rigid pattern of working hours that leaves practically no scope for individual choice. Rationalisation of individual and group behaviour has gone so far that it almost entirely eliminates spontaneity, initiative and imagination. The individual has in many cases ceased to have any influence on the timing and schedules of the work process. Yet these are among the main variables as regards his job and working conditions. This explains the strong reaction aiming at the removal of all avoidable constraints and at less standardised and more personal patterns of behaviour.

There is justifiable pressure to get rid of outdated or harmful forms and methods of work, and this has been partly responsible for the gradual introduction of new ways of organising work taking account, among other things, of progress in the behavioural sciences. Many believe that a revolution in attitudes to work is taking place and that it can only lead to a completely new framework for work.

The question that most are asking concerns the direction of change in conditions of work, i.e. new patterns of working time, improved pay systems, wider application of ergonomics, new and more imaginative ways or organising work, increased protection of the physical and social environment. Out of these various alternatives, it does seem that a loosening of the constraints so as to allow some degree of freedom to organise one's own working time is one of the best means of reducing the feeling of being a slave to one's work and improving the quality of working life.

## Working hours in present-day conditions

The growing significance of the time factor is leading to greater realisation of the new sociological and psychological dimensions of both working life and non-working life. These interact and are of equal concern to the individual so that they need to be studied together. Here, however, we shall only be dealing with the first aspect, in which working hours and the changes taking place in them occupy a central position.

Looking back, we can see how much the social and human aspects of working hours have changed. The main need is no longer to prevent excessive hours from being worked, but to deal with evils of a different kind due to the pace of modern life. Industrial and urban growth now force many workers to live in the suburbs. The increasing cleavage between work and home means that more time has to be spent away from the latter in connection with one's job, quite apart from the demands of the job itself - the fatigue of travel is added to the normal work fatigues.

The technological and economic aspects of the question have also changed - greatly. Technological progress has led to a spectacular increase in productivity. While this has made for shorter working hours, the high cost of modern machinery and plant and the need to make them pay for themselves quickly have led to shift working, with the advantages and disadvantages that this involves.

Finally - and this needs particular emphasis - there is the present tendency to view hours of work in a wider framework, since technological and scientific progress in various fields and the rate of change in modern life are making increased scale and larger units of measurement necessary. The time when hours of work per day and week were the sole concern is long past. We are moving towards the unit of the working year (allowing for vacations and public holidays) or, better still, the working life concept (allowing for the minimum age for employment and the retirement age).[1]

This account of the new features would be incomplete without a reference to the importance of the psycho-social framework in which people work and which has an influence on the pattern of hours of work. The framework is determined in part by the personnel structure (age, sex, marital status, family responsibilities, and the proportion of workers who are handicapped, foreign or country-dwellers) and in part by the effects of business fluctuations and structural factors.[2]

All this goes to show that, in present conditions, the problem of working hours goes beyond the setting of statutory limits, and involves also the scheduling and distribution of hours in accordance with two principles, i.e. a relaxation of standard patterns and a degree of freedom of choice, accepted by society and regarded as basic to job satisfaction.[3]

A further effect of the changed character of the time factor can be seen in the relationship between the planning of working hours on one side, and the pattern of school hours and town and country planning on the other side. The arrangement of hours in and out of school affects not only the children but also their teachers, the parents and the whole population. The school calendar affects the timetable for family and work-related activities, travel and leisure. Conversely, work schedules have an impact on school timetables. And the repercussions of the different patterns of working time on town and country planning are obvious. For example, a change-over to a working day with only a short midday interruption enables housing to be further out and more dispersed. Again, the introduction of flexible hours, longer work-free periods and individual choice of rest days leads to an easing of traffic problems and more efficient use of public transport and recreational facilities.

---

[1] Grossin describes life as essentially "a temporal experience": Les temps de la vie quotidienne (Paris and The Hague, Mouton, 1974), p. 15.

[2] See W. Grossin: "La structure des durées de travail et les influences conjoncturelles dans 14 branches d'activité industrielles de 1955 à 1964", in Revue française des affaires sociales (Paris, Jan.-Mar. 1967).

[3] See Final Report of the International Conference on New Patterns for Working Time (Paris, OECD, 1973).

Experience to date shows that the different approaches to the scheduling of working time are inter-related and complementary. It has been noted, for example, that the adoption of flexible daily hours is followed sooner or later by demands for more flexible schedules over the week, month or year.[1]

## New patterns of working time

In industry, the new approach has been reflected, in some cases, in the scheduling, staggering and co-ordination of working hours, and in other cases, in a more or less free pattern over the day, week, year or even over the individual's working life. Some of the new arrangements apply to groups of workers; others are based on a choice freely made by individuals. They have been adopted for various reasons, some deriving from sociology and the psychology of human needs, and others from economic necessity or simple recognition that adjustments have to be made in every type of society.

The real significance of the new arrangements comes out most clearly if they are viewed as ways of making work more worth while and improving the quality of living, in a strategy for humanising the individual's working life.

The new approaches can be considered according to units of time -

1. As regards the working day, they may consist of -

(a) a compressed working day;

(b) staggering of the set hours;

(c) individual choice between alternative timetables offered by management;

(d) flexible working hours subject to certain conditions and limits.

2. The working week may be compressed into 5, 4 1/2, 4 or even 3 days.

3. As regards the working year, efforts are made to stagger annual holidays.

4. As regards the individual's whole working life, the new approach regards the age for starting work and the age of retirement as flexible, and allows for substantial amounts of recurrent education during working life as a means of achieving greater social equality and as a catalyst in the improvement of the social environment.

We shall therefore consider in turn: reduction of hours of work, the compressed (or undivided) work-day, the compressed work week, staggered working hours, flexible working hours, part-time employment, staggered annual leave and the prospects for a new pattern of the individual's working life.

---

[1] See Jacques de Chalendar: Vers un nouvel aménagement de l'année (Paris, La Documentation française, 1970), and L'aménagement du temps (Paris, Desclée de Brouwer, 1971).

## II.  REDUCTION OF HOURS OF WORK

### General remarks

Among the main advances made in the field with which we are concerned, the reduction of hours of work must be mentioned first.

It is recognised today that increased productivity makes it possible to reduce working hours.  Experience has shown that moderate reductions, if carried out by stages in a methodical fashion, do not lead to a parallel drop in productivity and production, as they oblige companies to reorganise, streamline their production and work methods, and increase their fixed capital.  It has also been shown that hours in excess of a given figure - for example nine hours a day - are not worth while, since they lead to a fall-off in labour productivity.

The reduction of working hours is perhaps best regarded not as a way of improving the pattern of working time but as a point of departure for developments that are qualitative in character.  For most of these, it is in fact an essential prerequisite.

The reductions in hours of work reported in this chapter are to be understood in the commonly accepted sense of a decrease in the number of hours without a corresponding decrease in wages. The kind of reduction in hours with a proportional reduction in salary that occurs in periods of economic slow-down or in the case of part-time employment is something different.[1]

### Recent advances

Considerable strides have been made in reducing working hours since the Second World War, and particularly in the last 25 years. A recent ILO study takes stock of the situation up to 1973.[2]  It shows that substantial changes in working hours had occurred in the preceding 20 years in all but 7 of the 27 countries surveyed.[3]  The number of exceptions was even lower if France was excluded, and especially the United States, where the position had been by no means stationary, as will be seen later.  Most of the reductions had been effected by stages from the 48-hour week to the standard 40-hour week or near it (44, 42 1/2, 42, 41 3/4, 41 hours).

---

[1] For a definition of part-time employment, see Chapter VII.

[2] See Evans, op. cit.

[3] Australia, Austria, Belgium, Bulgaria, Canada, Czechoslovakia, Denmark, Finland, France, German Democratic Republic, Federal Republic of Germany, Hungary, Ireland, Italy, Japan, Luxembourg, Netherlands, New Zealand, Norway, Poland, Spain, Sweden, Switzerland, USSR, United Kingdom, United States, Yugoslavia.

A comparison of hours of work per year in different countries shows that here, too, marked progress has been made. According to a report submitted to the OECD International Conference on New Patterns for Working Time (Paris, 1972) and covering the period 1958-72, standard hours of work were (in general or in many cases) below 2,000 in 14 out of 20 OECD member countries, as compared with only 6 countries out of 40 in 1958.[1]

With the collapse of the boom of the 1960s, the period of rapid change and much experimentation came to an end. But the impetus that it gave is continuing, though progress is slower and irregular, taking different forms and being based on different motivations. The later developments (whether in a limited field or of a more general scope) that have occurred in spite of the current recession are significant because they are typical of the long-term evolution rather than short-term trends, which are influenced by transitory factors. What is important and what we shall try to do is to identify those features that are likely to set a higher standard or to become a more or less permanent principle. This will be attempted by examining cases of action taken or planned at the national or regional level and for particular industries or groups of workers.

In Belgium, the 40-hour week and a four-week annual holiday became general in 1975 as a result of joint efforts by employers and workers. The Government had only to approve the decisions previously taken by the social partners.

In France, the working week was reduced from 45.3 hours in 1959 to 43 hours in 1974. By 1 January 1976 average working hours in all sectors were 41.8 per week. Discussions on further reductions are in progress as part of an effort to improve over-all conditions of employment and to mitigate the effects of the recession.

In Japan, the results of an annual survey of 5,000 firms in the manufacturing and service sectors, published by the Ministry of Labour, showed that the average work week per worker covered by the survey was 42 hours, 21 minutes. In large plants with over 1,000 employees, two-thirds of the workforce worked fewer than 40 hours per week.

In the United States, the 40-hour week has in many cases been reduced since the 1960s to about 35 hours, with a substantial increase in the length of the annual vacation and the number of legal holidays. An expert group commissioned to forecast the situation with regard to fringe benefits for the period 1970-85 predicted further progress during that period.

Sweden provides some very interesting examples, which in some respects foreshadow the shape of things to come. Weekly working hours for the economy as a whole were reduced by collective agreements and legislation to 40 by the beginning of the 1970s, and the social partners agreed that shift work should be reduced to 36 hours per week. Fresh discussions are now in progress on a further reduction in working hours. The principal demand of the workers' organisations is for a 6-hour day and a 30-hour week, their long-term aim being to ensure equality between men and women workers as regards household tasks, including child rearing.

---

[1] See D. Maric: "Picture, country by country and branch by branch, of the actual duration of time worked", Supplement to the Final Report of the International Conference on New Patterns for Working Time (Paris, OECD, 1973), p. 23.

In Norway, weekly hours for shift workers were reduced in 1975 from 40 to 38, and a further reduction to 36 was made in April 1976.

The Ministers responsible for labour questions in the EEC countries recently adopted a recommendation for the 40-hour week with a four-week annual holiday with pay to be adopted by all the countries by the end of 1978. It also recommended that the weekly hours should normally be distributed over five days only, with variations in certain sectors where this is not feasible.

It is also worth mentioning that the European Confederation of Trade Unions at its second regular congress (London, April 1976) included in its suggested remedies for unemployment and inflation a proposal for a 35-hour work week and five weeks of holidays with pay in all European countries.

Without attempting to cover all the reported reductions in hours (some of which are only minor), it is interesting to compare progress in more detail in the manufacturing sector. The European metal trades may be taken as an example. Figure 1 shows that, starting approximately in the 1960s, the principal stages in the reduction of the work week were when hours were set at 44, 43, 42 1/2, 42, 41 1/4, 41 and 40, and that these points were reached in the different industrial countries within only a few years of each other.

Let us now examine a particular case, that of Canada, which is revealing in other respects. The current 40-hour week has been practically the same for the past 20 years. In view of this long period of immobility it is the long-term evolution that is of interest. It is expected that the recent interest in the compressed working week and in flexible working hours will ultimately reinforce the drive towards a reduction in working time; so far, however, where these have been tried out they have not led to any changes in the total number of hours worked. The future standard most frequently advocated is a 4-day week of 32 hours, and there appears to be a firm conviction that working hours will continue to decline.[1]

The reduction in weekly hours in Canada over the period 1947-72 is shown in figure 2. The over-all reduction has been appreciable, from 45 to just over 40 hours per week. However, two periods of unequal length can be noted: the first showing a steep fall from 1947 to 1956 or 1957, and the second showing a fairly flat curve from then to 1972. One explanation of the latter is that Canadian workers prefer higher earnings, or leisure time in the form of longer annual leave or a larger number of statutory holidays, to a shorter working week. This preference for substantial periods of leisure was reflected in the 1960s by a marked increase in the length of the annual vacation and the number of statutory holidays, which accounted for two-fifths of the total reduction (estimated at 50 hours) in annual working time in that decade. Another possible explanation is one advanced in a recent study made in the United Kingdom,[2] which suggests that reductions in

---

[1] Canada Department of Labour: Information, 5 Sep. 1974; and Trends in working time, June 1974.

[2] See M. A. Bienfeld: Working hours in British industry: an economic history (London, Weidenfeld and Nicholson, 1972).

Figure 1.  Dates of reductions in the standard work week established by law or collective agreements (starting-point 45 hours weekly) in the European metalworking industry

| Weekly hours | 45 | 44 1/2 | 44 | 43 3/4 | 43 1/2 | 43 | 42 1/2 | 42 | 41 3/4 | 41 1/2 | 41 1/4 | 41 | 40 |
|---|---|---|---|---|---|---|---|---|---|---|---|---|---|
| Germany, Fed. Rep. of | 1.10.56 | | 1.1.59 | | | | 1.1.62 | | | | 1.1.64 | | 1.1.67[1] |
| Austria | 1.2.59 | | | | | 1.1.70[1] | | 1.1.72[1] | | | | | 1.1.75 |
| Belgium | 1956/57 | | 1.5.66 | | | 1.10.68 | | 1.7.70 | | | | 1.1.72 | 1.1.73 |
| Denmark | 1.3.60 | | 1.3.66 | | | | 1.6.68 | | 1.9.70 | | | | 2.12.74 |
| Finland | 1957 | | | 1966[2] | | 1967[2] | | 1968 | | | 1969[2] | | 1.1.70 |
| France | | | | | | | | | | | | | 1936 |
| Italy: (a) iron and steel | 1.1.64 | | 1.1.65 | | | 1.7.65 | 1.11.68 | 1.5.69 | | | | 1.1.70 | 1.1.71[3] |
| (b) motor vehicles and aviation | 1.1.65 | | 1.7.65 | | 1.11.68 | 1.5.69 | | 1.1.70 | | | | 1.1.71 | 1.1.72 |
| (c) mechanical and electrical | 1.11.68 | 1.5.69 | | | | | 1.1.71 | 1.1.72 | | 1.1.72 | | | 1.12.72 |
| (d) shipbuilding | 1.5.69 | | 1.1.70 | | 1.1.70 | | | | | | | | 1.12.72 |
| Luxembourg: (a) metalworking | | | 1.1.71[4] | | | | | | | | | | 1.1.75[4] |
| (b) iron and steel, non-ferrous metals | | | 1.4.56 | | | | | | | 1.1.68 | | | 1.1.72[5] |
| Norway | 1.3.59 | | | 1.7.67 | | 1.1.62 | 1.1.64 | | | | | 1.1.70 | |
| Netherlands | 1961/62 | | 1.1.47 | | | | 1.7.68 1.7.70 | | | | 1.1.74[6] | | 31.12.74[6] |
| United Kingdom | | | 28.3.67[7] | | | | | | | | | 1.12.64 | 5.7.65 |
| Sweden | 1.1.60 | | 1.5.63 | | | | 1.1.69 | | | | | 1.7.71 | 1.1.73 |
| Switzerland | 1.5.60 | | | | | 18.3.68[7] | | 1.3.60 | | | | | 1.1.73 |

1 Effective from first Monday in January 1970, 1972 and 1975.  2 In winter, the 45-hour week remained in effect: in summer, an increasing number of weeks comprised 40 hours: averages over the year were 1966: 13 weeks; 1967: 21 weeks; 1968: 30 weeks; 1969: 39 weeks.  3 One additional day off every eight weeks from 1 January 1973.  4 Statutory hours.  5 Taking account of statutory holiday entitlements (42 days of annual holiday plus 10 public holidays).  6 The enterprise may make the whole reduction from 41 1/2 to 40 hours as from 1 July 1974 instead of in two stages as shown.  7 1967: 44 hours 10 minutes; 1968: 43 hours 20 minutes.

Source:  Union des industries métallurgiques et minières:  Conditions de travail dans la transformation des métaux européenne (Paris, Feb. 1975).

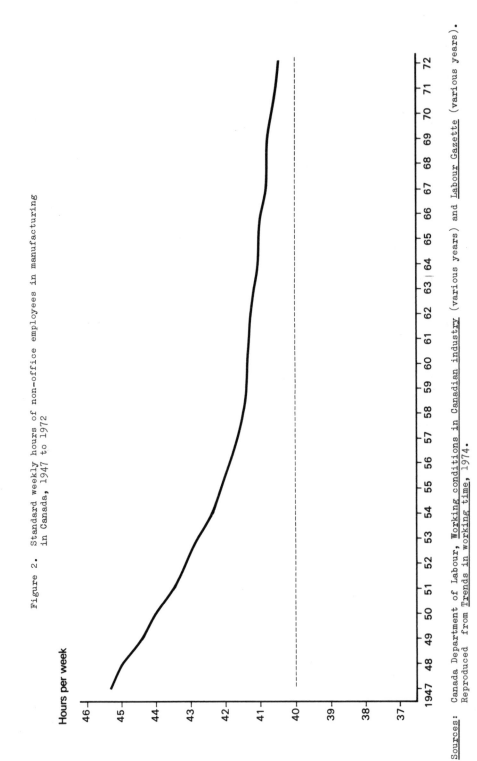

Figure 2. Standard weekly hours of non-office employees in manufacturing in Canada, 1947 to 1972

Sources: Canada Department of Labour, Working conditions in Canadian industry (various years) and Labour Gazette (various years). Reproduced from Trends in working time, 1974.

working hours occur at irregular intervals over a long time span.
The peaks are separated by plateaux, that is, periods during which
there is little action, if any, or pauses before the onward drive
regains momentum - strengthened, it might be added, by accumulated
reserves of productivity.   It has been noted that, in Britain,
hours have fallen by one-third in the period since 1850 (from 60 to
40 hours a week) and that each reduction took place in a period of
one to three years around 1871, 1919, 1948 and 1964.

## III.  COMPRESSION OF THE WORKING DAY

The earliest of the innovations in the pattern of working hours is the replacement of the two-part day, with employees going home between morning and afternoon work, by a work day with only short breaks, including one for lunch.  Although this has meant a departure from social and family custom and eating habits, the travel and fatigue involved in a double journey to and from work each day has become too great for any other solution in modern conditions.[1]

A typical example would be a work day beginning at 7 a.m. or 8 a.m. and ending at 3 p.m. or 4 p.m., with a short break in the middle of the day for a light meal at or near the workplace.  The main meal is taken after work, whenever most convenient in relation to other spare-time activities.[2]

The system was adopted earlier and is most widespread in the English-speaking and Scandinavian countries, but is also gaining ground elsewhere.

It is interesting to note that the idea dates back to the beginning of the industrial age.  Panckouke, writing in 1780 on "How to increase the happiness of part of the nation without harming anybody" proposed that all business should be conducted between 8 a.m. and 5 p.m. with only a substantial breakfast at about 11 a.m.[3]

### Advantages and disadvantages

There are a number of advantages both for the employer and for the workers, together with some benefits from the point of view of the economy as a whole.

A first and significant advantage is that, by compressing working hours and reducing "warming-up" time,[4] the unbroken work day tends to increase productivity.  It also tends to increase job satisfaction by giving employees more scope for leisure pursuits and for family and social life, and this is reflected in higher individual output and easier recruitment.  It may enable the firm to make some savings in overheads, e.g. lighting and heating.

---

[1] A study made in the 1960s in France showed that 42 per cent of employees were absent from home for over 12 hours (Comité national pour un aménagement des temps de travail et des temps de loisirs (CNAT)).

[2] In France, for example, the noon break ranges from three-quarters to one hour.

[3] Jacques Derville:  "Par l'aménagement des horaires de travail, suppression des pointes, agrément de l'existence", in Transmondia (Paris), May 1964.

[4] Derville (op. cit., p. 16) reports that experiments made by some insurance companies suggested a saving of about 20 minutes per employee per day.

From the point of view of the individual worker, apart from the daily gain in free time which many of them value more than the reduction of weekly hours, there is the reduced risk of accident from having only one instead of two return journeys to make. The change-over to a light meal in the middle of the day is considered to be beneficial to health in present-day conditions. In addition, the unbroken work day makes it easier to improve the distribution of working hours over the week by compressing them into fewer days.

From a wider point of view, its main advantage is that it enables hours to be staggered within a given area or occupation.

Nevertheless, there are also some disadvantages and points of criticism. For employers, it often means additional investment in canteens or restaurants and possibly other facilities (e.g. day nurseries) or at least a contribution to their cost. For workers, those who would still be able to go home at midday or who attach particular importance to the traditional dinner with the family will have to make a sacrifice. There is also the question whether, in the case of work involving considerable physical or nervous strain, the short midday breaks allows enough time for recovery. In the local environment, the change may affect public transport services owing to the drop in users.

## Conditions for the change-over

The change to an unbroken day can only be made when all have agreed to it, since resistance by a minority can greatly harm its smooth functioning. It also presupposes the existence of certain basic facilities, such as a canteen or restaurant on the premises, or restaurants in the vicinity. The best solution is of course a company restaurant, but it is also the most expensive since premises have to be provided and relatively large outlays are entailed. The company, in such cases, normally assumes the costs of kitchen equipment, dining hall furnishings and salaries of restaurant personnel. An alternative is the issue of meal tickets, financed in part by the company, to enable company employees to obtain moderately priced meals at small restaurants in the neighbourhood with which special arrangements have been made. In some instances - but these appear to be rare - the company contracts for meals with a catering firm.

The facilities needed may go further than what can be provided by the company. If working women are to be able to accept the unbroken work day, they must be relieved of the obligation of providing their children with a midday meal. This means that school canteens must be set up and a series of other steps taken to ensure that they can function smoothly.

## IV.  THE WORKING WEEK

Another way in which the pattern of working time is changing is through the fall in the number of work days in the working week. Since the 5-day week can now be regarded as a common arrangement, the expression "compressed work week" is being used to denote a shorter week of 4, 3 1/2 and even 3 days.

In theory, a shorter work week can be produced by flexible working hours, since credit hours earned during previous working days can be taken as time off at the end of the week or at the beginning of the following week.  However, we are here concerned with compression of the working week into fewer than five days, independently of any other change in the arrangement of working time.

### The compressed work week

The compressed work week reflects the tendency of contemporary industrial societies to look for better ways of combining social and economic aims.  It gives practical expression to the preference for more extended leisure periods over a reduction in daily or weekly hours, and also for greater variety in working schedules.

The compressed work week that is now being experimented with comes at the end of a period of accelerating change.  The traditional 6-day week, for centuries regarded as immutable, gave way after the Second World War to the 5 1/2-day week, which in turn was regarded as the ideal for several decades.  However, with the speed of technological advance, rising productivity and the consequent demands of labour for its share, the 5-day week became a universal objective.[1]  And at the present time, even before the 5-day week has become the general practice, a 4 1/2-day week, a 4-day and an even shorter week are being tried out.  The present analysis focuses on the 4-day week, which appears to have the widest appeal as compared with other intermediate and perhaps temporary solutions.

To avoid misunderstanding, it must be made clear that the 4-day week normally means that the same weekly number of hours are compressed into four days, and not that their number is reduced. It thus involves many social and economic problems that have not yet been finally solved, chiefly because experience with it has been too limited in scope and time.

---

[1] It may be recalled, as a matter of interest, that it was Henry Ford who first introduced the 5-day week in his automobile plants in about 1920.  At the time this was regarded as a scandalous innovation, flouting every established tradition.  Its opponents even cited the Bible in support of their argument that man must work six days and rest on the seventh.  See Jean-Pierre Hogue: "L'horaire variable: quelques conséquences", in L'aménagement des temps de travail, op. cit., pp. 97-98.

It is already apparent, however, that the 4-day week offers appreciable advantages for all concerned. For workers, it means a 3-day week-end, fewer journeys to and from work, and greater opportunities for vocational training. The first reports also show a decline in absenteeism. For management, it means a more intensive use of plant and equipment, with a resulting lowering of costs (heating, lighting, maintenance, etc.); moreover, repairs can be done without interrupting the production process. As for its broader economic repercussions, the 4-day week would appear to stimulate the labour market and to attract persons looking for part-time employment. It also creates additional demand for capital goods and services connected with leisure activities, which in turn generates more employment opportunities.

The compressed work week is of interest also from another point of view. Its effect is very marked on the cycle of work and rest in shift work. By providing more free days, it increases the number of normal-pattern days and so makes adjustment easier after night shifts.

However, the often excessive length of the working day tends to produce a slackening of effort and a consequent decline in productivity. It may therefore be concluded that the advantages and disadvantages of the 4-day week are in direct relation to the number of weekly working hours.

Having said this much, the question arises whether the 4-day week constitutes genuine social progress. When a company is working at full capacity in several successive shifts - which is made easier where the unbroken work day is in operation - the volume of production may increase substantially. But this also creates physiological, psychological and social problems that cannot be disregarded.

Once the principle of compressing the 5-day week had been accepted, a number of arrangements could be tried out. In the United States, several companies have experimented with a 7-day week, manned by two shifts, each working 3 1/2 days and 36 hours weekly, but paid for 40 hours.[1] Other companies have introduced a 37 1/2-hour week, worked in 3 days of 12 1/2 hours each. Still others, particularly banks and insurance companies, are prepared to introduce a 3-day week of 12 hours daily. However, the initiative in such extreme cases has come mainly from companies that rely heavily on data-processing, because costly computers must be kept in continuous operation and manned by as many shifts as that requires.

## Experience in different countries

In the United States and Canada, the compressed work week was first tried out in the early 1970s. By mid-1971 some 600 firms in

---

[1] See International Organisation of Employers: Information Bulletin, No. 3 (Geneva, 1971).

the United States had experimented with it in one form or another for at least some weeks in the year, mainly on the basis of a 4-day week of between 10 and 9 hours (daily hours were shorter where the 4 1/2-day week was introduced). An estimated 75,000 persons were affected, or approximately one in every 1,000. By 1973 the number had risen to an estimated 3 million. In Canada about 200 firms, nearly 100 of them in the Province of Ontario, were running similar experiments during the same period.[1]

Experience up to 1971 showed that the plan had mostly been introduced in small- and medium-sized firms, generally after a trial period, though there were some larger firms, such as the John Hancock Mutual Life Insurance Company employing about 6,000 persons at its Boston headquarters alone.

From the most recent reports, moreover, it appears that today, several years since the 4-day week was welcomed as a revolutionary step opening the way to a new era of leisure, only 2 per cent of full-time wage earners work fewer than five days a week. This percentage includes persons on 3-day, 3 1/2-day, 4-day and 4 1/2-day weeks, normally made up of at least 35 working hours. The 5-day week is prevalent where weekly working hours total between 35 and 45 and is most widespread in sectors where the normal total is 40. The current status of the 4-day week has some resemblance to that of the 5-day week in the 1920s, but there is no certainty that it will become standard in the proper acceptation of that term.[2]

In Europe, the first experiments go back to the 1960s. A small British firm, Roundhay Metal Finishers, at Batley in Yorkshire, introduced a compressed working week for its 40 employees in 1965. In the Federal Republic of Germany, the first to adopt a 4-day week was a publishing firm, Herbert Riesler, in Hamburg, in 1967. In France, one case was reported of a 4 1/2-day week introduced in 1972; the firm concerned, situated near Grenoble, employed mainly women, and the workforce had already accepted the system of an unbroken work day.[3]

Experience with the compressed work week in Britain is limited as in most other European countries, even though 4 1/2-day and 4-day weeks were fairly common in the early 1960s among shift workers in the British engineering and textile industries. According to Sloane, wherever the compressed work week has been tried out, employers have been generally satisfied: there have been

---

[1] See United States Department of Labor, Janice Neipert Hedges: "A look at the 4-day workweek", Monthly Labor Review (Washington, US Government Printing Office, Oct. 1971), p. 33. See also Bernard M. Tessier: "La semaine comprimée de travail: progrès ou anachronisme", in L'aménagement des temps de travail, op. cit., pp. 137-147.

[2] See United States Department of Labor, Janice Neipert Hedges: "How many days make a workweek?", Monthly Labor Review (Washington, US Government Printing Office, Apr. 1975).

[3] La Tribune de Genève, 12 Jan. 1972 and 3 Oct. 1973.

improvements in labour recruitment and reductions in turnover.
Few data are available, however, on increased productivity.  On
workers' attitudes, Sloane reports that 70 per cent of the workforce in the three firms he surveyed considered the compressed
week an improvement in that it gave them a longer week-end and
more opportunities for leisure activities, and necessitated fewer
daily journeys to and from work.  However, a sizeable minority
maintained that it was difficult to readjust to work after the long
week-end break, and some found that they were more tired as a result
of the long work periods.[1]

It is not always easy to assess the real impact of the various
features of the compressed work week.  It may therefore be useful
to consider a particular case, that of a mechanical engineering
firm in the United States, which introduced a 4-day week in April
1969.  The firm manufactured grinding machines and the work was
therefore dirty, noisy and monotonous.  Hence, although located in
an area with one of the highest unemployment rates in the country
(6.8 per cent), the firm was finding it difficult to recruit labour.
It therefore introduced a 4-day week of 36 hours instead of 40, but
with no corresponding decrease in pay.  At first overtime was
maintained, but was soon found to be unprofitable owing to the
length of the working day:  output in the tenth hour amounted to
only about 40 per cent of normal output.  Overtime was therefore
abolished and an additional work shift employed instead.  The
results were very encouraging.  Between April 1969 and October
1970 production rose by 14 per cent, and absenteeism declined by
54 per cent.[2]  In the euphoria of these first results the management concluded that the system was universally applicable;  however,
as will be seen, others disputed that view.


## Limitations


The findings from a few years of experiments with the compressed work week cannot be conclusive, but they suggest that there
are a number of problems, some of them serious enough to cast
doubt upon the validity of the compressed work week.

The main objection is the excessive length of the working day,
which could affect the health and the physiological and psychological well-being of the workers concerned;  it is therefore
argued that there must be a reduction in hours at the same time.
The 5-day week itself only became possible because of a reduction
in weekly hours.

---

[1] See P. J. Sloane: Changing patterns of working hours,
Department of Employment, Manpower paper No. 13 (London, HMSO, 1975),
pp. 4-5 and 20-27.

[2] Union des industries métallurgiques et minières: Documentation étrangère, No. 279 (Paris, Oct. 1971), p. 2 (quoting from a
report published in the New York Times Magazine).

From the sociological point of view, the impact of the compressed work week is twofold: at work and away from work. At work, an excessively long day is likely to affect the social and psychological atmosphere, to hinder communication between management and the workforce and to reduce the time that can be devoted to union affairs. Away from work, the sharp change in the daily ratio of work to leisure is liable to impair the worker's relations with his family and his social environment. On the other hand, the compressed work week adds a further dimension to the problem of leisure as a result of the increased number of days off.[1]

The expected economic benefits from the compressed work week, particularly in increased productivity and reduced labour costs, are not confirmed by the latest information. Measured over a longer time-span, no steady trends in this respect are apparent.

Various other objections have been voiced. Some fear that a working week of three or four days will lead to double job-holding (moonlighting) with the undesirable social, physiological and economic consequences that this entails. Others feel that the striking novelty of the 4-day week may divert attention from the main issue - improving the status and quality of working life.

The spread of the 4-day week appears to have suffered a serious setback in 1971 with the failure of collective bargaining for a pilot project at one of the plants.[2] Quite a few companies have changed their minds since. The reasons most frequently given are that absenteeism, after an initial drop, returned practically to its previous level; that productivity gains were less than expected; and that fatigue caused by long working hours created new problems of defective workmanship and work-related accidents. According to a study by the American Management Association, 240 out of 3,000 firms that had introduced a 4-day week since 1970 had already returned to the standard 5-day week.

Tessier gives some interesting recent data on the trend in Canada. On the basis of a survey made by a management consultancy firm in Toronto in November 1973, he points out that, among the organisations which had not adopted the compressed work week, the percentage still in favour fell from 90 to 62 between 1972 and 1973, and the percentage opposed to it rose from 10 to 32. On the other hand, among organisations that had tried the compressed work week for 12 months or more, 89 per cent were still for it in 1973 and only 9 per cent against it. As regards the effects on worker morale, productivity, absenteeism and labour turnover, the survey showed no substantial change after 12 months' experience or more in 80 per cent of the organisations covered.[3]

---

[1] See Tessier, op. cit., pp. 158-167.

[2] *Financial Times*, 15 Dec. 1971.

[3] See Tessier, op. cit., pp. 151-152.

The compressed work week has been so little used in European countries that no conclusion is possible as to the attitudes of the workers. However, a survey carried out by the Allensbach Public Opinion Institute in the Federal Republic of Germany found that replies varied with age rather than sex or level of education. Among workers under 30 years of age, 55 per cent were in favour of a 4-day week and 38 per cent in favour of a 5-day week. Workers between the ages of 30 and 44 were fairly evenly divided. Older workers preferred a 5-day week. It is also interesting to note that supervisory, clerical and semi-skilled employees, unlike the skilled workers, showed no particular interest in a compressed work week, and were indeed more inclined to oppose it.[1]

Finally, there does not seem to be much enthusiasm for the compressed work week among the trade unions. The Canadian Labour Congress issued a statement opposing it and calling instead for a work week of four days of eight hours each.[2] In the United Kingdom, where the normal working week of manual workers was on average 40 hours in April 1974 and overtime raised this to an average working week of 46.3 hours, the unions were prepared in some cases to accept a compressed week in exchange for abandonment of systematic overtime provided this did not affect the level of workers' output or earnings, but in general wanted a shorter week only if normal weekly hours are also reduced.[3]

---

[1] Le Monde, 10 July 1971, which cites Die Welt, Hamburg.

[2] See Tessier, op. cit., p. 156.

[3] See Sloane, op. cit., p. 5.

## V. STAGGERED WORKING HOURS

### General remarks

The effects in terms of traffic congestion of having much the same times of work in factories, shops and offices have been obvious for a long time. The need to provide for a very large volume of transport at peak hours when workers go to and return from work involves heavy cost to the economy. The difficulties of travel are also a source of physical and nervous tension affecting not only the workers themselves but also the population as a whole. When factories, offices and shops all close at about the same time, it is very difficult for people to attend to necessary personal business outside working hours.

This state of affairs has led to attempts to stagger working hours within firms and among firms in a town or industrial area. There are thus two forms: internal staggering of hours within a company to reduce queueing and parking difficulties at the start and finish of the working day, and external staggering of hours in different firms in an area or town.

Internal staggering can be conveniently considered with flexible working hours. This chapter is therefore concerned with external staggering where offices, workshops and factories in an area stop work earlier, while shops and government offices keep to their existing hours or close later. This allows the vast majority of employees to do their shopping or deal with formalities after work. Travel becomes easier as traffic peaks are levelled off, and there is an appreciable saving in physical and nervous fatigue.

Work hours staggered in this way could make considerable savings on public transport by allowing a more rational utilisation of vehicles. In London, for example, it was estimated that 3,500 buses were needed to carry passengers in the middle of the day, whereas 5,500 were needed at peak hours.[1]

This mass movement to and from work has become a major worry for town planners and a nightmare for the people themselves. Some believe that the only lasting solution will be through decentralisation of employment; but this depends upon an increasing number of economic and social variables and is outside the scope of the present study.

Some figures from a study[2] on Greater Paris give an idea of the problem at its worst. In 1901 only 100,000 persons worked outside their home borough. This figure grew to 448,000 in 1926, 975,000 in 1954 and 1,166,000 in 1962. The increase was, moreover, out of

---

[1] See Sloane, op. cit., p. 31.

[2] Made by the French National Statistical and Economic Research Institute (INSEE).

all proportion to the increase in the active population: whereas
daily journeys to and from work rose by 348 per cent between 1902
and 1926, by 117 per cent between 1926 and 1954 and by 19.5 per
cent between 1954 and 1962, the increase in the working population
in the same periods was only 26.7 per cent, 9.7 per cent and 10.8
per cent respectively. The strain which this imposes on the
working population represents the social cost of the failure to
plan the use of land and time more efficiently. Another point
that emerged was that workers in Greater Paris spent 14 per cent
of work hours solely on travel to and from work.[1] In Greater
London, average journey-to-work time in 1972 has been estimated at
29 minutes.[2]

## Experience in different countries

The first experiment with staggered working hours appears to
have been carried out in 1955 in Metz (France). It had been
found that the number of vehicles in the town's public transport
system that were not operating during the greater part of the day
was more than three times the number needed for a regular normal
flow of the service. The extra vehicles were used only to carry
passengers at the peak periods when everybody went home for lunch
at noon and left again for work or school at 2 p.m. Estimates
based on the rate of population growth showed that the fleet of
vehicles would have to be further increased by a substantial
amount. It was decided that staggering of journeys both ways for
workers and for school children was needed if the available transport was to be properly used. Following a vigorous campaign,
agreement was reached and children started to go home and return
to school 15 minutes earlier than before, and factory, shop and
office workers 15 minutes later. The first tangible result was
that the transport corporation was able to save the price of ten
vehicles and did not have to raise fares.[3]

Other experiments were made in France two years later, for
example in Strasbourg and Dijon, after surveys directed by the
Productivity Commission in the winter of 1957-58. In Strasbourg
the change was made the other way round. Lunch hours for offices
were put back by 15 minutes. Those for schools were brought
forward by the same amount as it had been found that school children
liked to dawdle in the town instead of going straight home, where
they would in any case have had to wait for their parents' return.
The change of hours had other good effects. In Strasbourg,
traffic flowed more freely, there was a 37 per cent increase in
public transport users and there was no congestion despite a substantial increase in traffic. In Dijon the number of travel-
related accidents declined.[4]

---

[1] Le Monde, 2 June 1964.

[2] See Sloane, op. cit., p. 29.

[3] International Junior Chamber and Comité national pour un
aménagement des temps de travail et des temps des loisirs (CNAT):
Staggering of working hours: an action-planning manual (Paris, 1961).

[4] See Jean Hallaire: "Vers un étalement des horaires de
travail" (Paris, CNAT, 1958), p. 10.

Figure 3.  Traffic density in Strasbourg, 1957 and 1958

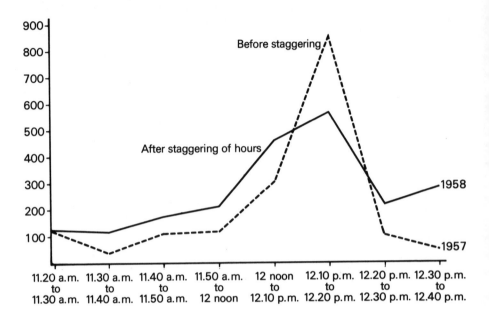

The graph shows the number of passengers recorded at 10-minute intervals on a tram service in Strasbourg.

Source:  International Junior Chamber and CNAT:  Etalement des horaires de travail - un programme d'action (Paris, 1961).


     Figure 3 illustrates the ebb and flow of passengers at 10-minute intervals in Strasbourg before and after hours were staggered.

     We have been speaking of the problems of scheduling of working hours in medium-sized towns;  they must be infinitely greater in huge conurbations like Paris, London or New York.

     When they are tackled, experience shows that all representative groups in the community must be consulted:  management and labour in factories, shops and offices, technical staff of the passenger transport companies, local authorities, etc.  In the search for solutions which represent the best compromise between the preferences and dislikes of different groups, it is often necessary to set up working parties of statisticians, economists, town planners, sociologists, doctors, psychologists and others to consider all aspects of the question.  Nor should it be forgotten that each city has its own individuality which must be taken into consideration in any prospective plans and solutions.

In the light of the different factors and interests involved, a study recommended the adoption of the following schedules for Greater Paris.[1]

| End of working day for employees in: | | Average |
|---|---|---|
| Manufacturing: single shift production workers .................... | 4.45 - 5.15 p.m. | 5 p.m. |
| Office personnel ...................... | 5.15 - 5.45 p.m. | 5.30 p.m. |
| Wholesale commerce, banking, insurance .......................... | 5.15 - 5.45 p.m. | 5.30 p.m. |
| Government offices ................... | 5.45 - 6.15 p.m. | 6 p.m. |
| Similar services directly dealing with the members of the public ............ | | 7 p.m. |
| Retail commerce excluding food shops . | | 7 p.m.[*] |
| Food shops ......................... | | 8 p.m. |
| Establishments providing personal services ........................... | | 8 p.m. |

[*] With possibly a later closing hour once a week.

Efforts to stagger hours in other countries have met with varying success. In the United Kingdom, a scheme worked out in Sunderland in 1957 has been fairly successful. In London, however, a number of attempts have been made since 1920 to stagger working hours but without much success. A committee for staggering working hours in Central London set up by the Minister of Transport in 1957 was able to persuade only a small minority of firms to introduce different hours. Of those that refused, 72 per cent thought that business efficiency would be reduced; and 23 per cent feared that staggered hours would make it more difficult to recruit and retain staff because employees objected to unusual starting and finishing times - which was surprising since it was common knowledge that "super peak" traffic occurred between 8.45 and 9 a.m. and between 5.30 and 5.45 p.m., and that working in London was considered as particularly tiring because of this.

By 1961, in spite of campaigns over a long period, only about 57,000 out of 1 million persons travelling daily to London, with journey-to-work times averaging over 30 minutes, were working staggered hours.[2]

In the United States, a breakdown of the working population by times of work in 1973-74 indicated travel peaks around 8 a.m. with 26 million persons involved (nearly two-fifths of the working population) and 4 p.m. with 37 million (over half the working population). The 4 p.m. peak was larger because 4 million other full-time or part-time workers began work at that time. The position is illustrated in figure 4.

---

[1] CNAT: _Le temps de mieux vivre_ (Paris, 1964).

[2] See Sloane, op. cit., pp. 5-6 and 29-33.

Figure 4.  Start and finish of working hours of all
United States workers, May 1974

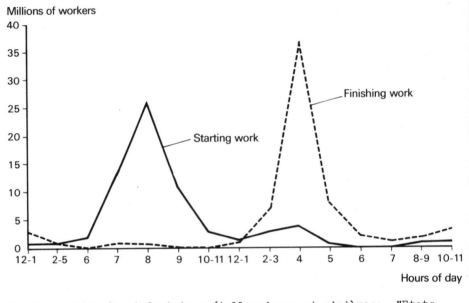

Source:  Union des industries métallurgiques et minières:  "Etats-
Unis - Le problème de l'étalement des horaires",
Documentation étrangère, No. 325 (Paris, Dec. 1975), p. 6.

This has naturally led to staggering of hours or the introduction of flexible working time as the only solutions.  In
Manhattan, for example, where traditional hours were 9 a.m. to
5 p.m., staggered hours starting and finishing 30 minutes earlier
or later have been in effect since 1970 in 400 firms, covering
220,000 workers, or some 60 per cent of wage earners.

Successful results have also apparently been achieved in
Washington, Tokyo and Osaka.

## VI. FLEXIBLE WORKING HOURS

### Main features of the system

Traditional ideas on the arrangement of working hours received a considerable shock when a regular system of flexible schedules was first introduced in some enterprises. It seemed likely to lead to a major change in the approach to hours of work. In the history of large-scale manufacturing few, if any, had ever supposed that these could be other than fixed hours laid down by the employer, apart from the special arrangements for commercial travellers, university teachers, etc., and those working in agriculture whose hours still vary according to the season, the length of daylight and the weather.

This is not the place for an account of the detailed working of the system of flexible hours and of its advantages and disadvantages, on which much has already been written.[1] The purpose of this chapter is to describe the latest developments and to assess the results.

A flexible hours system consists of a fixed "core" period when all employees are present, and flexible hours before and after, for which the individual has a choice as to when he will start and end his work day. He must do this in such a way as to average over each "settlement period" (normally a week or a month) a set number of hours as prescribed within the limits allowed by the law or collective agreement. There is a lunch break, which may be fixed, variable or included in the core time. The range over which individual starting and stopping times can vary is of course limited by the time during which the establishment is open. Hours worked in excess of the daily average (up to a permitted maximum) are set off against less than the average hours on other days. A credit or debit balance at the end of one accounting or "settlement" period may, within specified limits, be carried forward to the next period. In some cases, credit hours within up to an authorised maximum may be used as a day's or half-day's leave in the next period.

Naturally, there are many variations in the actual arrangements. Four of the most commonly used schemes are illustrated in figure 5.

The object of flexible hours is to give all employees a latitude comparable to that allowed in practice to management personnel, relying on their sense of responsibility. The system offers a substantial degree of freedom and marks a definite step forward in social progress.

The system has evolved considerably since it was first introduced, and a number of refinements have been made to take account of the differing needs and interests in particular cases.

---

[1] See, for example, Heinz Allenspach: Flexible working hours (Geneva, ILO, 1975).

Figure 5.   Some examples of core times and band widths in a
            flexible working hours system.

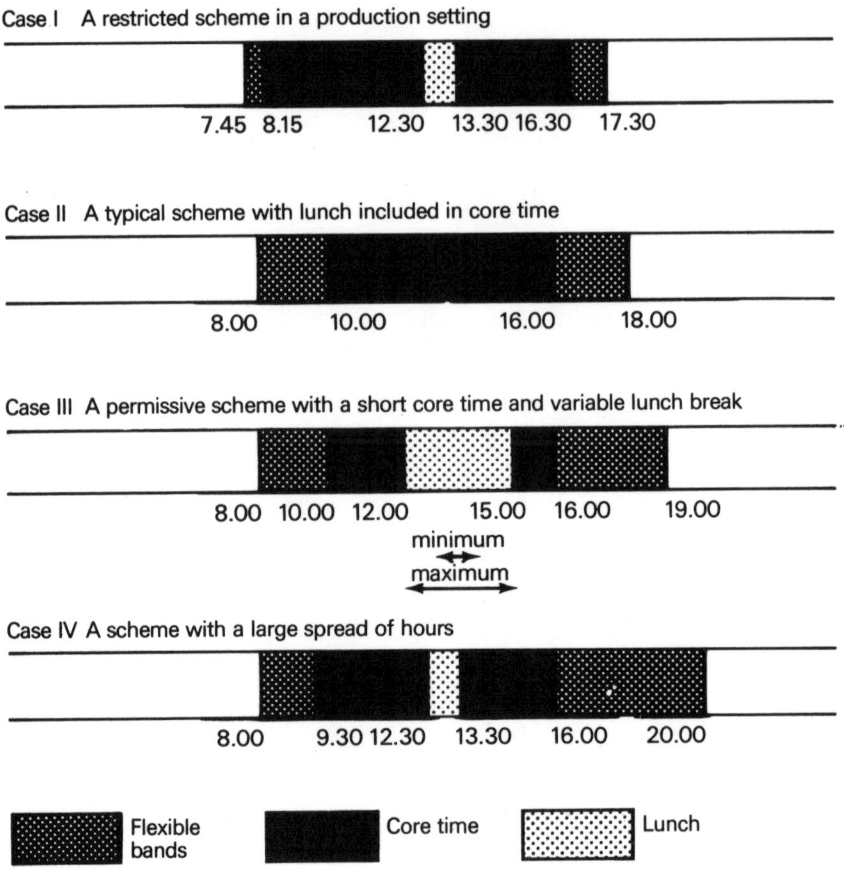

Case I   A restricted scheme in a production setting

        7.45  8.15      12.30  13.30 16.30   17.30

Case II   A typical scheme with lunch included in core time

        8.00        10.00          16.00      18.00

Case III   A permissive scheme with a short core time and variable lunch break

        8.00  10.00  12.00       15.00  16.00      19.00

                            minimum
                            maximum

Case IV  A scheme with a large spread of hours

        8.00      9.30 12.30   13.30      16.00      20.00

[ ] Flexible bands    [ ] Core time    [ ] Lunch

Source:   P.J. Sloane:  Changing patterns of working hours,
          Department of Employment, Manpower paper No. 13 (London,
          HMSO, 1975).

        The flexibility allowed as between one accounting period and
another and the carry-over of credit and debit hours also vary
from one scheme to another.  Sloane cites four types:  (1) flexibility restricted to the working day;  (2) flexibility within the
working week;  (3) flexibility within the month;  and (4) flexibility between months with two variants:  (a) where credit hours
can be used as time off but only outside core time;  and (b) where
they may be accumulated and taken as half-days or whole days off.[1]

_____

[1] See Sloane, op. cit., p. 9.

The Chalendar report, published in France in 1972,[1] distinguishes three alternative ways of providing a degree of freedom of choice:

(1) each employee chooses one of several alternative schedules offered by management, and this becomes his regular schedule;

(2) each employee chooses his own arrival and departure times in such a way as to include a period of compulsory attendance prescribed by management, and then keeps to these arrival and departure times for a specified period;

(3) each employee can each day choose his arrival and departure times, provided that he maintains an average number of compulsory attendance hours (so that the core time is in effect also flexible).

Significantly, the idea of flexible working hours arose out of an attempt to resolve two management problems: to facilitate the employment of women, who were seriously handicapped on the labour market by the rigidity of working hours, and to ensure a rational use of labour in the light of variations in the volume of work and transport difficulties. These economic considerations led Mrs. Kristel Kämmerer, an economist and management consultant in Königswinter (Bad Honnef) near Bonn, to develop the idea of a flexible schedule in 1965.[2] The social aspects of the scheme, with all its sociological and psychological implications, did not become apparent until later.

## Development of flexible hours schemes

According to most writers, the Messerschmidt-Bölkow-Blohm corporation in the Federal Rebpulic of Germany[3] was the first to introduce flexible working hours for a substantial proportion of the workforce. The idea developed and spread at an impressive rate in the space of a few years, and by 1973 it was estimated that 6 per cent of the labour force in the Federal Republic were on a flexible schedule. Information dating from 1975 indicated that one-third of firms and six out of every ten government offices had adopted flexible hours. The system appears, however, to have found widest acceptance of all in Switzerland, where it covers 30 to 40 per cent of all employees (or a total of 1,300,000 to 1,700,000 persons) and in some cities (e.g. Winterthur and Zurich) up to 70 per cent.

---

[1] See J. de Chalendar: L'aménagement des temps de travail au niveau de la journée. L'horaire variable ou libre. Rapport du groupe d'étude réuni à la demande du Premier Ministre (Paris, La Documentation française, 1972).

[2] Cf. Marie-Claire Boucher: "L'horaire variable du travail: anarchie ou désordre organisé", in L'aménagement des temps de travail, op. cit., p. 45.

[3] Flexible working hours may in fact have been in operation by 1965 or even by the beginning of the 1960s, when the scheme was first tried out in Switzerland. See Jean-François Baudraz: L'horaire variable de travail (Paris, Les Editions d'organisation, 1973).

The system has also spread, though at a slower pace, in other Western European countries, for example, Austria, Belgium, France, Italy, the Netherlands, the United Kingdom and the Nordic countries.

In Belgium, where a start was made in 1970, it has only very recently been adopted on any wide scale in manufacturing (especially in public enterprises). In France, an estimate in 1971 put the number of firms with flexible hours at about 15; a later estimate in 1975, however, gave a figure of at least 800 establishments in numerous sectors, particularly in public administration and social services. In the United Kingdom, flexible hours were likewise first introduced in 1971. By 1974, an estimated 500 organisations and institutions and 100,000 employees had opted for the system. At present it is chiefly found in insurance firms, local government and the public services, and mainly covers white-collar workers. In industry, it has been introduced by a number of pharmaceutical, food and tobacco companies.[1] The single largest experiment with flexible hours made by a single enterprise seems to be the one started by Fiat in Italy in 1973, which now covers 25,000 company workers.

To date, flexible hours may be regarded as a specifically European innovation, but the system has also been tried out in Canada, the United States and Japan, for example.

### Experience in different countries

The schemes that are being tried out in different countries are very varied, and study of their results is steadily increasing our knowledge of the factors involved so that improvements can be made and mistakes corrected.

The following pages are an attempt to pick out the main findings from some of the experiments. The findings quoted are of course drawn from case studies and in-plant surveys, since there are no official statistics that could be used.

In Belgium, a conference held at Diepenback in March 1974 made a first assessment of the results of the introduction of flexible working hours.[2] The exchange of views indicated that, for companies, the measurable benefits were mainly a decline in absenteeism and overtime, lower personnel turnover and fewer work-related and travel-related accidents. Other benefits that were more difficult or impossible to measure were a better atmosphere at work, greater motivation among the employees, better use of working time, better performance and, in general, a degree of job satisfaction. The specific benefits of flexible hours for the workforce were easier travel to and from work, adjustment of hours

---

[1] See Revue du travail (Brussels, March 1975); also Sloane, pp. 9-10.

[2] See Revue du travail (Brussels, March 1975).

to the pace of the individual, some relaxation of the feeling of being tied down by one's work, and a sense of greater indiviual freedom.   On the other hand, short absences for special reasons (for example, visits to the doctor, or urgent personal or family matters), which were accepted as part of normal working hours under the conventional system of fixed working hours, now had to be made up for by equivalent work time.   Another point was the drop in earnings resulting from the decline in overtime.

In Canada, it has been pointed out that, unlike the compressed work week, which is generally adopted by majority vote and may not meet individual needs, the flexible hours system permits individuals to select the hours that suit them best, so that there is nothing to prevent them from continuing with the former fixed schedule.   It has also been noted that, although flexible hours do not imply a reduction of working time, their introduction usually provides an opportunity for reviewing the position in regard to working hours as a whole.[1]   Flexible hours were instituted on an experimental basis in 1972 and 1973 in the public service and in some establishments in the services sector, and in each instance the overwhelming majority of those concerned favoured adoption of the new plan.

The idea of flexible hours is also gaining ground in Ireland. Few concerns in the private sector have as yet shown interest, but the public authorities recently announced their intention of introducing the scheme in government services.   At present the system is in operation in several insurance companies and for staff employees in perhaps a score of other companies.   At Glenn Abbey Ltd., a knitted goods manufacturer, about 30 workers in the data-processing department work flexible hours.   Here the initiative came from the workers themselves and not, as in most cases, from management. After a six-month trial period, 95 per cent of the department were in favour of continuing the scheme, and the management agreed with them because of the decline in overtime and absenteeism.   Judging by the replies of some other establishments to questionnaires, once a scheme is in operation, it is generally regarded as an improvement by employees and employers alike.   However, the trial periods revealed a number of problems in the matter of checking attendance.

In unionised firms, questions such as the degree of flexibility and the length of  the core period have normally been discussed with union representatives.   The maintenance of certain privileges, such as permitted absence for visits to the doctor, has been a matter for negotiation, as has the length of the lunch break.

Another interesting experiment with flexible hours took place at the Irish Productivity Centre (IPC) at the initiative of the management.   An unexpected move from the town centre to an area less easily reached involved a number of problems that could only be overcome by introducing flexible working hours.   Apart from the increase in daily travel time, workers were finding it more difficult to get a proper lunch (there were no restaurants near the new premises), to do their shopping, to go to the theatre, etc.

---

[1] See Canada Department of Labour: _Trends in working time_, 1974.

Experience so far with flexible hours in Ireland suggests that they will be introduced in the public service as a whole and will also spread in the private sector; however, they are unlikely to be applied to manual workers for some time.[1]

In Australia, the Labour Department conducted a survey on flexible working hours in October-November 1973 covering 20 undertakings in the public and private sectors. It also carried out a three-month experiment covering a small sample group (45 persons, of whom 27 were men and 18 women) working in three different areas of its central office in Melbourne. While many of the findings and conclusions of the survey[2] tallied with those reached in other countries, the results of the department's own experiment showed that, notwithstanding the size of the flexible periods and the range of choice in the matter of starting and finishing hours, by the end of the third month the participants tended to arrive and leave at about the same times as those prescribed under the former fixed schedule. The experiment was made using the following periods: spread of the working day, 8 a.m. to 6 p.m.; core time, 10 a.m. to 4 p.m.; flexible periods, 8 to 10 a.m. and 4 to 6 p.m.; lunch break, 1 to 2 p.m.[3]

In the United States, where the compressed work week appears to be preferred to other ways of rearranging working time, interest in flexible hours is nevertheless growing, particularly in the federal government services. Detailed information and conclusions on experiments with flexible hours are not yet available, but employers appear to feel that the advantages of the scheme outweigh its drawbacks. A report[4] covering 59 public and private employers that had tried flexible hours showed that two main systems were being used. In the first, adopted in 19 establishments, employees had to work the same number of hours each day but had some latitude in the scheduling of those hours; the working day was from 7 a.m. to 6 p.m. and core time from 10 a.m. to 3 p.m. Under the second system adopted in 40 establishments, the number of hours worked in a day could vary provided a prescribed number were completed each week.

---

[1] See "Flexible hours in Ireland", in European Industrial Relations Review, No. 20 (London, Aug. 1975).

[2] Details of the case studies will be found in Personnel Practice Bulletin (Melbourne, Australian Department of Labour, Dec. 1973), Vol. 29, No. 4, pp. 337-352.

[3] See Robyn Harkness: "An experiment with flexitime", Personnel Practice Bulletin, op. cit., pp. 327, 329 and 330.

[4] Virginia Martin: Hours of work when workers can choose, reported in International Herald Tribune, 12/13 July 1975.

Of the 19 establishments experimenting with the first system, 10 reported an increase in productivity and none a decline; 12 reported a decline in lateness and only one an increase; six a decline in absenteeism and only one an increase; two a decline in overtime and none an increase. On the debit side, six firms reported some increase in overhead costs resulting from the spread of the working day. Similar results were reported by the 40 other firms. Productivity had increased in 18, and none reported a decline; lateness and absenteeism had declined in 34 and 22 firms respectively, and no firm reported an increase. Overtime was reported by 11 firms, and an increase in overtime by two. Only three firms reported some increase in overhead costs.

None of the firms reported any major problems, except perhaps some difficulty in ensuring attendance in the early morning or late afternoon. On the whole, flexible hours seem to have been regarded as benefiting all concerned, especially those with considerable responsibilities outside their work.

In the United Kingdom, employers' impressions after experimenting with flexible hours have been generally favourable.[1] The surveys made so far have covered no more than a dozen firms or groups of firms, but employers reported a reduction in time-keeping losses and a quicker start on arrival at work. Most employers thought that the system had had little effect on productivity, but a sizeable minority mentioned some improvement and only a few mentioned a decline. In spite of the additional costs on time-recording procedures, none of the employers surveyed desired to return to fixed hours. Moreover, the anticipated difficulties in communication and co-ordination had not materialised.

As to employee reactions, flexible hours were generally regarded as an important innovation, permitting greater personal freedom and a better balance between private and working life. Despite differences in the percentage of favourable and unfavourable answers on particular points of detail (daily travel to work, for example, or time-recording methods), the over-all conclusion was that the advantages of the system largely outweighed its drawbacks; indeed, a large proportion of employees saw no drawbacks in the system at all. Suggested improvements in the schemes currently in operation centred overwhelmingly on even greater flexibility, i.e. a wider choice of starting and finishing times, reduced core time, greater flexibility in the lunch break and more provision for carrying over credit hours to take time off.

Trade union reactions have varied. Some unions, for example, the Association of Scientific, Technical and Managerial Staffs and the National and Local Government Officers' Association and the Association of Professional, Executive, Clerical and Computer Staffs, favour the adoption of flexible hours (with some reservations in the latter case). On the other hand, the Technical and Supervisory Section of the Amalgamated Union of Engineering Workers and the Society of Graphical and Allied Trades have strong reservations. The Trades Union Congress (TUC), for its part, issued a

---

[1] See Sloane, op. cit., pp. 7-20.

policy statement for its 1973 non-manual workers' conference
drawing attention to possible difficulties where flexible hours
were not applied to the workforce as a whole, but only to office
workers, and recommended that each case should be assessed in the
light of the employer's motives in introducing the system.

In a limited number of cases the experiment broke down for
lack of adequate preparation, or because it was too hastily
introduced.

By and large, the flexible hours system appears to be
spreading fairly rapidly in the United Kingdom.   Given the range
of organisations in which the system has been introduced, the
structure of the British labour force and the rapid growth of the
service sector, flexible hours may well become a feature of employment for up to 50 per cent of all workers.

In France, a number of interesting developments have taken
place in this sphere in recent years, not the least of which was
the passing of an Act dated 27 December 1973 on working conditions.
Section 16 of the Act provides that, at the request of certain
categories of workers, employers are authorised to depart from the
rule of common working hours and to adopt "individual" hours.
The scope of the law is very wide, covering industrial, commercial
and agricultural undertakings, government offices, the liberal
professions, non-profit-making organisations, trade unions and all
types of associations.   Three conditions are stipulated for the
introduction of individualised hours:  a request by the personnel;
absence of any opposition by members of the works committee or
personnel representatives;  and notification of the labour
inspector.

Some years earlier - in January 1972 - a working party, set up
at the request of the Prime Minister, had performed a useful service
in identifying and clarifying a number of problems under discussion,
including an analysis of various concepts in use ("individualised",
"personalised", "mobile", "free", and "variable" working hours).[1]

A second working party was set up subsequently to consider
the main problems that had emerged in the course of experimentation with the system.   The group's report,[2] found that the system
was generally appreciated by employees but gave a warning that it
could lead to an excessively long work day detrimental to workers'
health and safety.   It recommended that the working day should in
no case be allowed to exceed 10 hours and that the lunch break
should be at least 45 minutes.   It pointed out that, as stipulated
in the 1973 Act, flexible hours must only be introduced at the
request of the personnel and with the agreement of the works
committee.   It also stressed the importance of explaining the
system fully to those affected, and of making a thorough joint
study of the detailed implementation of the system with the
accredited representatives of the personnel.[3]

---

[1] See J. de Chalendar:  L'aménagement des temps de travail au
niveau de la journée.   L'horaire variable ou libre, op. cit.

[2] See L'horaire libre en 1974 (Paris, La Documentation
française, 1974).

[3] Notes rapides du ministère du Travail, No. 24 (Paris,
30 Sep.-6 Oct. 1974).

So far, the trade unions appear to view the system with some suspicion, feeling that there is a risk in some cases of the workers being losers from the system. During the meetings of the second working party, representatives of the major unions (CFTC, CGT, CFDT) made it very clear that flexible hours must not be introduced as a means of abolishing existing privileges or of diverting attention from more important matters such as working hours and other conditions, purchasing power, job security, transport facilities, etc. They also insisted that the introduction of flexible hours must not interfere with the right to organise and that union meetings must take place during core time and not during the flexible periods.[1]

### The lessons learnt

Considerable progress has been made both in the structure of the new system and in the way in which it is operated. It may therefore be useful to consider what lessons may be drawn from the experiments made to date.

A preliminary point that must be made is that, although flexible hours make it easier for individuals and groups (e.g. members of a shift) to arrange their working and non-working life and can be designed in various - often highly ingenious - ways, there are nevertheless very definite limitations. The freedom of choice that the system provides is not, and cannot be, total.

A number of alternative schemes have been mentioned earlier. As regards the justification for introducing flexible hours, the evidence from current schemes is that flexible hours are a definite step forward in human progress and that the participants greatly appreciate their new sense of freedom. In certain instances, the introduction of the system merely endorses existing practices.[2]

It is clear that, despite its numerous variants, the system cannot be applied indiscriminately in all sectors and services. Cases in point are continuous or semi-continuous operations, assembly-line work, i.e. any work which must be broken down into numerous, small operations or where the products cannot, because of their size or weight, be stored during the interval between one shift and another.

---

[1] See "Horaires libres", Les cahiers d'information du chef de personnel, No. 69 (Paris, Editions Contact, 1975).

[2] At Messerschmidt, the idea of staggering arrival times was prompted by the realisation that a period of 20 minutes must be allowed for all employees to park their cars in the morning. In Paris, in the 56-floor Maine-Montparnasse building, it was found that it took at least 45 minutes for the elevators to carry the 7,000 persons working there to their respective floors. In Brussels, flexible hours were introduced in 1970 in a big insurance company, La Royale Belge, because its offices had just been transferred to the outskirts, about 40 minutes' distance from the centre; some flexibility had to be allowed in arrival and departure times, particularly since many of the employees used public transport. See Le Monde, 2 Apr. 1975, and Revue du travail (Brussels, Mar. 1975).

On the other hand, in the services sector and especially in government offices, the introduction of flexible hours appears to present no difficulties. Indeed, the system appears particularly well suited to certain sectors (e.g. banking and insurance), as well as to certain types of occupation, such as accountancy, graphics, data processing and general office work.

Clearly, the shorter the working hours established by law or collective agreement the more favourable will be the reaction to a flexible schedule. In certain cases, where the law is so specific that it would interfere with the operation of flexible hours (for example, by preventing the debit hours from being set off against credit hours and compensation for additional hours in the form of time off) amendment of the law may be needed.

Reservations about this mode of scheduling working time still exist in various quarters. Some are afraid that it will create chaos or they simply object to innovations. Others, particularly supervisory staff, regard it as a threat to their position and authority. Some workers and unions fear that the new system, however attractive, may be used to avoid dealing with serious problems, or as an alternative to acceptance of other more important demands. There are also fears that flexible hours may interfere with union rights. Other problems are the maximum length of the working day, the minimum length of the lunch break, maximum hours for young workers, the spread of the working day, arrangements for credit and debit hours, etc.

Time recording is another sensitive issue. Various methods are used: attendance sheets, time-clocks, individual meters and systems using data-processing techniques. Experience to date shows that there are objections to the use[1] of time-clocks, and that individual meters are the most acceptable.

As far as we know, once flexible hours have been introduced, no one has asked for a return to fixed hours. Nevertheless, if the system is to succeed, certain preliminary steps have to be taken, the first of which is to inform and reach agreement with staff representatives on the procedures to be adopted for applying the proposed system. It is also advisable to proceed by stages, starting with trial periods.

With the development of the system, a number of problems of varying importance have come to light, some of them peculiar to particular undertakings: for example, choice of rest days and holidays, combination of statutory holidays with weekends and arrangements for the transport of employees by special buses. These problems are under study and in some cases have already been resolved.

---

[1] See Cahiers d'information du chef de personnel, op. cit., p. 46. In addition, L'aménagement des temps de travail, op cit., pp. 317-320, gives details of an individual meter developed by a company in the Federal Republic of Germany, which some regard as a major advance facilitating the spread of flexible hours schemes.

## VII. PART-TIME EMPLOYMENT

### Structure

Part-time employment is yet another way of adjusting working hours - in this case to meet the needs of those who would like regular employment if they are allowed to work for less than the standard hours.[1]  It is widespread in times of rapidly expanding business activity when demand for labour outstrips the normal supply, but it is also popular with various groups of the population and may be offered by employers in some fields of employment independently of business conditions.

There are a number of reasons for the spread of part-time employment.  Firms may offer it in order to make fuller use of plant, to increase output per worker, or to deal with shortages of semi-skilled workers.  Workers choose part-time employment because they want more latitude in using their time and in coping with present-day conditions in an industrial society.

There is marked interest in part-time work, not only among women but also among the young, the elderly and the handicapped. Students may have to work in order to be able to continue their studies.  Older people after retirement may wish - for financial or psychological reasons - to find a job that does not involve the strain of full-time work.  The handicapped may also need to work as far as they are able.  However, it is chiefly women, and especially those with family responsibilities, who are interested in working part time.

There are also circumstances in which any worker, whether a man or a woman, may at some stage need part-time employment, e.g. when obliged to turn to a new occupation because of technological change or because of commitments unrelated to his or her work.[2]

Another factor that has greatly contributed to the spread of part-time employment is the rapid growth of the service sector, in which there is a great deal of scope for such employment and which has absorbed a substantial number of workers from other sectors. According to Hallaire, the proportion of workers who have moved over to the tertiary sector in France, for example, is likely to represent 44.3 per cent of the active population in 1980, as

---

[1] Persons doing part-time work outside their normal work hours are not considered here, nor of course is involuntary short-time working.

[2] Jean Hallaire:  "Working hours per week and day", in Supplement to the Final Report of the International Conference on New Patterns for Working Time (Sep. 1972) (OECD, 1973), p. 107 and especially pp. 119-123.

compared with 28.6 per cent in 1960.[1]  A number of ILO committees
have drawn attention to the growing scale of part-time employment
in shops, offices, nursing and the civil service in their discussion
of conditions of work in those sectors.[2]

In the retail trade, part-time employment largely depends on
local conditions (supply and distribution structure, opening and
closing times, peak shopping days and hours), and makes it possible
to maintain proper sales service without excessive strain on the
staff.  In the public service and in nursing, the greater use of
part-time employees in recent years is primarily due to the policy
of making it easier for women to enter and re-enter employment.


## Development


The amount of part-time employment has grown substantially
over the last 10 years in most of the industrial countries (e.g.
Belgium, Canada, Denmark, France, Federal Republic of Germany,
Sweden, United Kingdom and United States), though the impact on
different sectors and trade and on union policies has not been
identical.

In Denmark, France, the Federal Republic of Germany and the
United Kingdom, most part-time workers are in the service sector.
For example, in a West German survey in the summer of 1971 covering
23 undertakings of different sizes in different sectors and parts
of the country, the proportion of part-time employees ranged from
0.5 per cent to 26.5 per cent, being highest in banks and insurance
companies (up to 14.2 per cent) and in department stores and chain
food stores (up to 25 per cent).[3]

In most of the countries concerned, particularly in Belgium,
West Germany, Sweden and the United Kingdom, the bulk of the part-
time workers were women.  In the United Kingdom, the 1966 census
showed over 2,500,000 women and about 350,000 men in part-time
employment;  and in manufacturing (June 1974) one in every four
women was employed part-time.[4]

---

[1] Ibid.

[2] ILO Advisory Committee on Salaried Employees and Professional
Workers, Seventh Session, 1974;  Joint Committee on the Public
Service, Second Session, 1975;  and ILO-WHO: Report on the Joint
Meeting on Conditions of Work and Life of Nursing Personnel, 1973,
Annex II.

[3] See Federal Ministry of Labour: Teilzeitarbeit in der
betrieblichen Praxis, Public Information Issue No. 53, Bonn,
Oct. 1973, p. 21.

[4] See ILO:  Part-time employment - an international survey
(doc. ILO/W.4/1973), p. 5;  also Sloane, op cit., p. 1.

In the United States, part-time employment has become wide-spread and is still increasing, mainly in department stores and supermarkets, as well as in business offices. In department stores, part-time workers are expected to outnumber full-time workers by three to one in the near future. In business offices, 2,139,000 persons were known to be working part-time in May 1971, 66 per cent of them women, these figures being higher than the figures for the retail sector.

There has also been a marked increase in part-time employment during the same period in industrialised countries elsewhere, for example in Australia and New Zealand.

## Arguments for and against

From the worker's point of view, the advantages of part-time employment are that it permits a choice between more work or more free time and offers the possibility of combining work with other personal commitments. It allows people to enter employment with-out having to give up personal and social activities that are part of their personality.

However, we must now consider the main arguments against the employment of part-time workers. To the extent that social over-head and service costs depend on the number of persons in employ-ment, the costs are proportionally higher in relation to part-time than to full-time workers. The fact that work responsibilities are divided between two personnel groups having a different status may create personnel management problems (e.g. in the organisation of work, job assignment and content), leading to more supervision and consequently increased cost. There is a risk of clashes due to friction between the two groups, and there are fears in some cases that part-time employment will upset the labour market and create pressures threatening the position of full-time workers.

The attitude of trade unions is on the whole negative, though they do not object to part-time employment in special circumstances. The main disadvantages in their view are that part-time workers are employed only in subordinate jobs and have no guaranteed rights, that the employment of part-time workers may impede or delay accept-ance of the major improvements demanded by labour (such as reduced working hours and higher pay), that it virtually excludes any opportunity for promotion, and that it endangers full-time employ-ment when the amount of work contracts.

## Outlook

The scope for the development of part-time employment depends, of course, upon a number of factors, such as current pay, social security and taxation systems and the facilities for vocational training and retraining.

If part-time employment is to be acceptable from a social and economic point of view, however, it must include certain guarantees under the law or collective agreements as regards job security, fair remuneration, weekly hours of work and other generally accepted advantages in employment, including the right to participate in the general life of the enterprise. Specific provision for part-time workers to receive family allowances and health, disability, old-age and unemployment benefits is also needed. Problems arising under social security as regards admission of part-time workers to existing schemes, entitlement to benefit and rate of benefit must be overcome, since it is almost impossible for part-time workers to meet some of the conditions for entitlement (e.g. length of employment and contribution period).[1]

There is no doubt that the flexibility provided by part-time work arrangements is attractive in industrial countries where the desire for greater freedom of individual choice is constantly growing. It must be recognised, however, that any increase in part-time employment will mainly depend on population trends, on economic and technological progress which determine the number and nature of the jobs to be filled, on employment policies in regard to the different classes of workers and population groups, and on the degree to which society as a whole accepts the principles of the right to work, job security and full participation in all spheres of life, both public and private, without discrimination of any kind.

---

[1] Cf. ILO Committee of Experts on Social Security: "Women and social security in Latin America" (doc. CSSE/D.5, 1975).

## VIII.  IMPROVING THE ANNUAL PATTERN

The annual pattern of working and non-working time may be modified in various ways.  Average hours of work may be calculated over longer periods, as in seasonal activities.  Additional days of time off with pay may be allowed in the course of the year, reducing the annual total of work days.  Flexibility in work-time arrangements for part-time or temporary employees, or for employees released for spells of recurrent education, are also of course a departure from the standard pattern.

This chapter is concerned, however, with a very tangible and important improvement, namely staggered annual holidays.


### The problem


The trend towards longer annual holidays with pay and the development of tourist travel into a full-scale industry have led to such congestion in the customary holiday months that there is a widespread desire for improvement in the quality of the holiday.

The dimensions of the problem can be illustrated most vividly by taking France, which is an extreme case.

Whereas in 1925 rather less than 40,000 industrial workers had an annual holiday under the terms of the collective agreements, in 1962 over 12 million adults (most of whom will have been employees) are known to have taken the holiday away from home - over half of them during the month of August.[1]  A survey for the period 1 October 1972 to 30 September 1973 showed that practically one out of every two went away for a holiday.  The average annual increase in the number going away on holiday at least once a year was 3.3 per cent, of which only 1 per cent was accounted for by population growth.[2]  Moreover, most of the holidays are concentrated in the two months of July and August.  Apart from this concentration in time, there was also a concentration in space:  in the 1960s, 40 per cent of vacations went to the same six départements of France.

---

[1] CNAT:  Pour des vacances plus heureuses (Paris, Mar. 1963), p. 3.

[2] INSEE:  Les vacances de Français en 1973, Series M, No. 41 (Paris, Feb. 1975), p. 7.  The annual surveys of the Institute showed the following percentages going away on holiday:  1964, 43.6;  1969, 45.0;  1973, 49.2.

Figure 6.   The summer holidays calendar

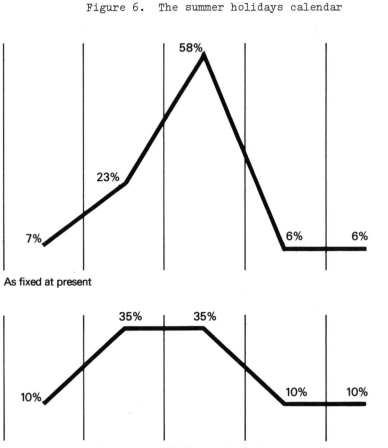

As fixed at present

As people would have preferred (1962 French Public Opinion Institute survey)

As holidays could be arranged (if the National Committee's suggestions are followed)

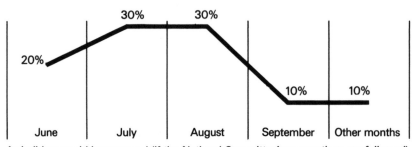

Source:   <u>Pour des vacances plus heureuses</u>, op. cit. (Paris,
          CNAT, 1963).

Three graphs based on a survey in 1962 (see figure 6) provide an interesting comparison of when the French took their holidays, when they would have preferred to take them, and when they could have taken them if certain proposals were followed.

An even more instructive picture at the same period is given in figure 7. This shows very striking differences, as between the countries covered, in the extent to which industrial production was affected by departures on holidays in August. For example, it fell from the annual average to two-thirds of this (100 to 66.5) in France, whereas over 80 or 90 per cent of production was maintained in the other countries given.

## Experience in different countries

Mass holiday travel reflects new aspirations arising out of a higher level of economic and social development. Studies have shown that holidays away from home increase with urbanisations, with changes in social and occupational status and with rising living standards. Apart from custom, the possibility of staggering annual holidays is limited by three kinds of factors: (a) the climate of a country and the length of its summer; (b) the duration and timing of school holidays; (c) the need to maintain production, stocks and deliveries, etc.

The material available on six countries makes it clear that, while there is congestion of summer holidays, the extent and urgency of the problem varies from one country or region to another, depending on climate, town and country planning, school programmes, the needs, customs and tasks of the population, the way in which the economy is organised, etc. There is naturally a great difference between the position in Mediterranean countries which are large "producers" of tourist services and the more northerly countries which are predominantly consumers.

After France, which has already been described, Belgium seems to be the country with the least staggering of holidays. The main holiday period is in July and August when the weather is warmest, with shorter holiday periods at Christmas (two weeks) and Easter (10 days). Efforts have so far been directed to changing attitudes through publicity stressing the advantages of holidays in June and September from the point of view of cost, service and amenity, rather than towards staggering the closing of factories or school holidays.

In the Netherlands, the authorities have for some years been pursuing a policy aimed at relieving the congestion in July and August. The policy, which has had the full support of the trade unions, is to co-ordinate annual holidays with the school calendar. Primary school holidays start on the last Friday in June and last for six weeks. During this time, unmarried workers are not given leave, and married workers with children take their holidays (two weeks, as a rule) in one of three successive periods. This sytem has operated successfully because there has been close co-operation between parents and school authorities.

Figure 7.   Percentage of industrial production maintained in
            August in six European industrialised countries

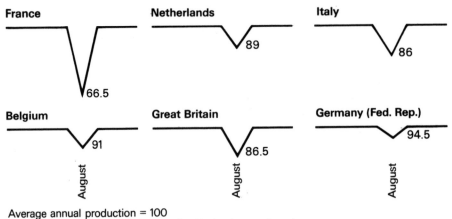

Average annual production = 100
(Institut national de la statistique et des études économiques)

Source:   Pour des vacances plus heureuses, op. cit.


        In Britain, the number of establishments closing down in
July or August is not very great and workers therefore have greater
choice in the timing of their annual holiday.   Nevertheless, the
concentration in those two months is very great, in view of the
warmer weather, tradition, and the fact that the school holiday
period in the summer is from late July to mid-September, which
allows less spreading than in countries with a longer school
holiday period.

        In Sweden, tourism is confined to the winter resorts, and
most of those who go away for their holiday take it abroad.   Any
staggering of holidays (in which the Government does not intervene)
is the result of a transfer of holidays from summer to winter,
rather than from spreading them over the summer months.   In 1969,
26 per cent of the major enterprises reckoned on one week out of
the four weeks of annual leave to be taken in the winter.   As
between a general close-down and close-down of plants in rotation,
the great majority preferred a short, general close-down to a
longer period of operating at less than full capacity.   A study
made of the country's big employers showed that only five used the
rotation system, four of them using it for periods of up to six
weeks.   Among the firms closing down completely, the monthly
percentages were as follows:

| Week | Percentage |
|------|------------|
| 22 June   - 29 June | 1.3 |
| 29 June   -  6 July | 6.7 |
|  6 July   - 13 July | 74.7 |
| 13 July   - 20 July | 97.3 |
| 20 July   - 27 July | 94.7 |
| 27 July   -  3 August | 82.7 |
|  3 August - 10 August | 20.0 |
| 10 August - 24 August (two weeks) | 2.7 |

In the Federal Republic of Germany, there is less tendency for all workers to go away in July and August.  One reason is that there is no season that is outstandingly favourable as regards the weather, and the enjoyment from a holiday is much the same at any time between mid-May and mid-October.  Another is that the different states (Länder) in the Federation are responsible for fixing school holidays and consult each other, so that in practice there is a staggering of annual holidays by date and region, thus giving a fairly balanced distribution over the year.

In the United States there has been a clear trend in recent years for the annual vacations with pay laid down in 96 per cent of all collective agreements to become longer.  The clauses normally provide for a system of staggering based on seniority. American experience is of particular interest because of the size of the country, the federal structure of states with their own laws and a great variety of climates (some with mild weather all the year round) and the mobility of the population.  In addition, there is the role and influence of the trade unions, which operate mass tourist facilities on a large scale, especially in Florida and California.  Whenever collective contracts come up for renewal, procedures for the summer closing of firms and the staggering of holidays are decided by agreement between unions and employers. The practice of sabbaticals, originally introduced in the teaching profession, and of long-service leave for highly skilled workers, further contributes to the spacing out of departures.

The combination of these different factors has brought about an automatic staggering of holidays, which is also made easier by the devolution of responsibility for education to local districts, which are able to make decisions in the light of the needs and interests of the local community.

To sum up, congestion at the time of the annual summer holidays is the result of three main factors:  (a) preference for the warmest part of the year;  (b) the timing of school holidays; (c) workplace arrangements.  The first can be influenced by the development of leisure activities at other times, e.g. winter sports and other activities for which other seasons are at least as good.  As regards the main school holidays, there seem to be

two practices:  (i) holidays of moderate length (e.g. seven weeks)
starting at staggered dates, and (ii) longer school holidays (nine
weeks or more) during which the parents' holidays can be staggered.
As regards the third factor, the arrangements may be affected by
the nature of production or services and by the proportion of
married people in the workforce;  where establishments cannot be
kept going while part of the personnel is on holiday, the close-
down periods may have to be staggered by inter-firm arrangements.
These factors interact:  for example, the longer annual leave
periods now available to workers give more scope for taking the
annual holiday by instalments, thus allowing more people to use
the available holiday accommodation during the most favoured time
of year.

## A NOTE ON LIFETIME DISTRIBUTION OF WORKING TIME

The boundaries of an individual's working life are the age of admission to employment and the age of retirement. In practice, people start work somewhat later than the minimum age (the European average in 1965-70 was 17 years 1 month, and the North American was 18 years 4 months). There is also a varying proportion of people who retire later and some who retire earlier than the pensionable age.

Between these two ages, total working time varies according to the length of the working week, the volume of overtime, the length of rest periods and holidays, the time spent on training or study during the working years, and periods of leave for special reasons (such as maternity).

The current trend within this pattern is towards a less clear-cut division between the formative years, time in employment and the years of retirement, so as to give the individual more scope for finding the best balance between work, further study, leisure and rest.

How large are the amounts of time devoted to each of these, how do they relate to each other and what proportions should they bear to each other? These questions lead on to the idea of a "time budget" applying not merely to each day or week but also to one's whole working life.

One interesting idea arising out of the study of patterns of working time is that of an integrated insurance system replacing the many existing schemes for income maintenance when people are not working. "Drawing rights" under the system would enable people to make use of income maintenance resources productively for study, training, general education, labour education or learning a new job. In addition to allowing lifetime freedom of choice and transfers of income from one period to another so that credit could be given for education before entering employment (for example), the system would also help to even out fluctuations in the economy.[1] If looked at from this angle, educational leave becomes an important factor in human resources development and an instrument of employment policy.

Finally, the total number of hours worked in the course of a lifetime might be one of the social indicators, to be read in conjunction with the economic indicators when analysing and evaluating the economic and social position in a country.[2]

---

[1] See Gösta Rehn: "Prospective view on patterns of working time", in Supplement to the Final Report of the International Conference on New Patterns for Working Time (Paris, Sep. 1972), op. cit., pp. 47-48.

[2] See Archibald A. Evans: Flexibility in Working Life (Paris, OECD, 1973), p. 104.

## CONCLUDING REMARKS

In this brief survey of recent developments in the distribution of working hours, we have seen that hours of work are now being approached in qualitative terms, since they affect the pattern not only of working time but also of non-working time - in other words, the lifetime pattern of the individual. Since the new trends developed at a time when economic activity was at a very high level, their future direction seems likely to depend on continuing economic growth and a steady increase in productivity - which were the factors creating additional income usable for a further rise in the standard of living or for improving the quality of life. Experience shows that, once a certain level is reached in the satisfaction of material needs, people tend to look for the kind of quality of life which they have always felt they needed and desired.

This explains the innovations in the arrangement of working time that are being so keenly debated. The choices eventually made will no doubt vary in different countries and according to local custom, levels of income and education, sex and family circumstances.

The new approaches directed towards the satisfaction and welfare of individuals, groups or the whole population, i.e. flexible hours, staggered hours, part-time employment, staggering of holidays and the lifetime pattern of working time are conducive to job satisfaction and enrichment, and encourage feelings of solidarity and responsibility. They clearly represent a further stage in social progress. They are tackling problems arising out of industrialisation and over-rapid urbanisation by seeking to free the individual from needless restrictions and to replace an authoritarian system by a consensual one allowing people to shape their own lives with due regard to the general interest. In different ways that are nevertheless complementary, the approaches are leading to a relaxation of traditional practices and opening up new horizons limited only by the need to maintain productivity, employment, good working relationships and the public interest.

None of the innovations is a panacea. Though they are interrelated, each has its particular characteristics, advantages and drawbacks. To be effective, they must be a joint effort made after careful consideration of all the alternatives and of all their short-term and longer-term repercussions. In the past, decisions to reduce working time by lowering the retirement age, lengthening holidays, prolonging the period of school education or shortening the working week have generally been taken in isolation without much consideration of the difficulties which each individual measure may create in other areas. It is therefore useful to put them side by side in order to obtain an overall view of a question which, as we have seen, lies at the centre of working life.

# BIBLIOGRAPHY

## Books

Allenspach, H.: <u>Flexible working hours</u> (Geneva, ILO, 1975).

Baudraz, J.-F.: <u>L'horaire variable de travail</u> (Paris, Les Editions d'organisation, 1973).

Baum, S. J., and Young, W. McEwan: <u>A practical guide to flexible working hours</u> (London, Kegan Page, 1973).

Bienfeld, M. A.: <u>Working hours in British industry: an economic history</u> (London, Weidenfeld and Nicolson, 1972).

Bolton, J. H.: <u>Flexible working hours</u> (Wembley, Middlesex, Anbar Publications, 1971).

CATRAL: <u>La pratique de l'horaire variable</u> (Vincennes, Guy Rabourdin, 1973).

Chalendar, Jacques de: <u>Vers un nouvel aménagement de l'année</u> (Paris, La Documentation française, 1970).

  - <u>L'aménagement du temps</u> (Paris, Desclée de Brouwer, 1971).

  - <u>L'aménagement des temps de travail au niveau de la journée. L'horaire variable ou libre</u> (Paris, La Documentation française, 1972).

Chalendar, Jacques de, and Lamour, Philippe: <u>Prendre le temps de vivre</u> (Paris, Editions du Seuil, 1974).

Dankert, C. E., Mann, F. C., and Northrup, H. R.: <u>Hours of work</u> (New York, Harper and Row, 1965).

Département des relations industrielles de l'Université Laval: <u>L'aménagement des temps de travail</u> (Quebec, 1974).

Evans, A. A.: <u>Flexibility in working life</u> (Paris, OECD, 1973).

  - <u>Hours of work in industrialised countries</u> (Geneva, ILO, 1975).

Grossin, William: <u>Le travail et le temps (horaires, durées, rythmes)</u> (Paris, Editions Anthropos, 1969).

Hallaire, Jean: <u>L'emploi à temps partiel</u> (Paris, OECD, 1968).

Hill, J. M.: <u>Flexible working hours</u> (London, Institute of Personnel Management, 1973).

Le Vert, P.: <u>L'étalement des activités - travail, transport, loisirs</u> (Paris, Fayard-Mame, 1972).

Mencier-Visser, Y. F.: <u>Le travail à temps partiel</u> (Paris, Tema-Editions, 1975).

Poor, R., and Samuelson, Paul A.: <u>4 days, 40 hours - reporting a revolution in work and leisure</u> (Cambridge, Mass., Bursk and Poor Publishing, 1970).

Saso, Carmen de: The four-day work week (Chicago, Ill., Public Personnel Association, 1972).

Sloane, P. J.: Changing patterns of working hours, Department of Employment, Manpower paper No. 13 (London, HMSO, 1975).

Tega, V.: Les horaire flexibles et la semaine réduite de travail (Montreal, Ecole des hautes études commerciales, 1973).

Wheeler, K. E., Gurman, R. and Tarnowieski, D.: The four-day week - an AMA research report (New York, American Management Association, 1972).

Zumsteg, B. J.: L'horaire libre dans l'entreprise (Neuchâtel, Delachaux et Niestlé, 1971).


Periodicals and documents

Brassington, William E.: "Is the 5-day week finished?", in Civil Service Review (Ottawa), Vol. 45, No. 2, June 1971.

Brulin, M.: "La réduction de la durée du travail et la croissance de l'industrie allemande 1954-1967", in Economies et sociétés (Geneva), Vol. 3, No. 12, Dec. 1969.

Bulkeley, William: "Four-day week poses problems for US industry", in the Guardian, 8 May 1973.

Derville, Jacques: "Par l'aménagement des horaires de travail, suppression des pointes, agrément de l'existence", in Transmondia (Paris), May 1964.

Elbing, O. A., Cadon, H., and Gordon, J. R. M.: "Time for a human timetable", in European Business (Paris), autumn 1973.

Grossin, William: "La dimension psychosociale de la durée du travail", in Revue française de sociologie (Paris), 1967.

   - "La structure des durées de travail et les influences conjonc- turelles dans 14 branches d'activité industrielles de 1955 à 1964", in Revue française des affaires sociales (Paris), Jan.-Mar. 1967.

Hallaire, Jean: "Staggering of starting and stopping times: the break-free day; part-time work", in Supplement to the Final Report of the International Conference on New Patterns for Working Time (Paris, OECD, 1973).

Harkness, Robyn: "An experiment with flexitime", Personnel Practice Bulletin, Vol. 29, No. 4 (Melbourne, Australian Department of Labour, Dec. 1973).

Hedges, J. N.: "A look at the 4-day workweek", Monthly Labor Review (Washington DC), Oct. 1971.

   - "How many days make a workweek?", Monthly Labor Review (Washington DC), Apr. 1975.

Maric, D.: "Picture, country by country and branch by branch, of the actual duration of time worked", <u>Supplement to the Final Report of the International Conference on New Patterns for Working Time</u> (Paris, OECD, 1973).

Ministry of Transport and Civil Aviation: "Rush-hour travel in Central London", Report of the first year's work of the Committee for the Staggering of Working Hours in Central London (London, HMSO, 1958).

OECD: <u>New Patterns for Working Time</u>. <u>Final Report</u> and <u>Supplement</u> (Paris, 1973).

O'Mally, B., and Salinger, C. S.: "Staggered work hours in Manhattan", <u>Traffic Engineering and Control</u> (New York), Jan. 1973.

Poor, Riva: "Social innovation: 4 days-40 hours", <u>Columbia Journal of World Business</u>, Vol. 91, No. 6 (New York), Jan.-Feb. 1971.

Simeray, J. P.: "Durée du travail et productivité", <u>Hommes et techniques</u> (Paris), Jan. 1965.

Willat, Norris: "Flexitime at Sandoz", <u>European Business</u> (Paris), autumn 1973.

"Can the four-day week work?", <u>Management Review</u> (New York), Sep. 1971.

Union des industries métallurgiques et minières: "Etats-Unis - comment combattre l'aliénation à l'usine", <u>Documentation étrangère</u> (Paris), Dec. 1972.

"Etats-Unis - le problème de l'étalement des horaires", <u>Documentation étrangère</u>, No. 325 (Paris), Dec. 1975.

"Flexible hours in Ireland", <u>European Industrial Relations Review</u> (London), No. 20, Aug. 1975.

"Flexible hours: it's about time", <u>Harvard Business Review</u> (Cambridge, Mass.), Vol. 52, No. 1, Jan.-Feb. 1974.

"Horaires libres", <u>Les cahiers d'information du chef de personnel</u> (Paris, Editions Contact), No. 69, 1975.

"Hours of work when workers can choose", <u>International Herald Tribune</u>, July 1975.

Ente Nazionali Idrocarburi (ENI): <u>Il problema dello scaglionamento delle vacanze</u>, Dec. 1970.

Les vacances des Français en 1973 (Paris, INSEE), Series M, No. 41, Feb. 1975.

<u>L'étalement des vacances</u> (Paris, La Documentation française, Sep. 1972).

"L'horaire libre", Hommes et techniques (Paris), No. 366, Apr. 1975.

"Moving towards the four-day week", Information Bulletin (Geneva,
    International Organisation of Employers), No. 3, 1971.

Pour des vacances plus heureuses (CNAT, Paris), Mar. 1963.

"Prevalence of the 5-day week in American industry", Monthly Labor
    Review (Washington DC), Vol XXIII, No. 6, Dec. 1926.

Rapport sur l'aménagement du temps, "Environnement" series (Paris,
    La Documentation française, 1976).

"Répercussions éventuelles d'une réduction de la durée du travail",
    Revue internationale du travail (Geneva, ILO), Vol. LXXIV,
    No. 1, July 1966.

"Short workweek has short life at Chrysler", Iron Age, 23 Dec. 1971.

Canada Department of Labour: Trends in working time, June 1974.